BLUE BUMS

The truth about mixed race babies from a mixed race baby

by Tendayi Ohorn

Copyright © 2021 (Tendayi Oborn)
All rights reserved worldwide.

No part of the book may be copied or changed in any format, sold, or used in a way other than what is outlined in this book, under any circumstances, without the prior written permission of the publisher.

Publisher: Inspiring Publishers,
P.O. Box 159, Calwell, ACT Australia 2905
Email: publishaspg@gmail.com
http://www.inspiringpublishers.com

 A catalogue record for this book is available from the National Library of Australia

National Library of Australia The Prepublication Data Service

Author: Tendayi Oborn
Title: Blue Bums
Genre: Children's Literature
ISBN: 978-1-922618-75-7

THIS BOOK BELONGS TO:

_____

Will the baby be born black?

My name is Arnja and I have a little brother named Ruslan.

My mum told me that before I was born everyone was wondering what colour I would be because my mum is black, and my dad is white.

My mum told me that people would often ask her if I would be born black or if I would be born white?

When I was born my skin was white like my dad's skin. My mum told me that she was scared to take me out of the house because she was afraid people would think that she had stolen me because my skin was so different to hers.

A few months after I was born, my skin gradually changed colour and it became darker.

I now have caramel coloured skin, which is a beautiful blend of black and white.

My skin darkens in the sun and lightens in the cold.

Can I touch your hair?

Everywhere I go people often stop and stare at my hair. My mum constantly gets comments about how different my hair is and people often want to touch and feel it. I don't like it when people touch my hair without asking for my permission.

When my hair is dry it is like my mum's hair, it rests in very tightly coiled curls and stands on end in the biggest afro.

When my hair is wet it is like my dad's hair, it is silky, soft and my tight curls unravel into straight long hair. When my hair is wet, it is easy to detangle and style.

I love being half black and half white because I can wear my hair in so many different styles. I wear my hair in braids like my mum does or I can pull my hair into a ponytail when I go to ballet.

What is it like having a black mum and white dad?

Our family is like any other family. My Dad is very big and strong. We play sports together. My Dad has taught me how to kick a ball and how to catch a ball. He has also taught me how to wrestle. My Dad and I often race, and I always end up on the floor laughing because we have so much fun. My mum loves to sing and wear bright colours. We often dance to her favourite songs. My mum is very loving and gives me and Ruslan lots of kisses. She loves hugging me and taking me to the shops. People always stop my mum to ask her where we are from. My mum likes to meet new people and enjoys telling them about our family. My mum and dad are different colours but love us just the same.

What is it like having family in two different parts of the world?

I come from two cultural backgrounds and share two different sets of histories. I am from the land of lions, elephants, rhinos, cheetahs, and buffalos but I am also from the land of kangaroos, emu's, wallabies, koalas and possums. I identify with both my backgrounds. I feel very special to be able to feel at home in Africa and at home in Australia. In Africa, I am an African and in Australia I am an Australian.

I am sure if you investigate your past, you will discover that you are made up of a mixture of places. We are all different, but we are also all the same.

Who are your friends?

I have friends from lots of different countries. I love all of my friends because when we play together, you cannot tell that we've all come from different places and share different histories. My friends are from all over the world. Some of my friends speak different languages. It's so nice to mix with people from different cultures. I love that we all look different and sometimes even sound different but that's what makes us interesting. I love listening to my friends when they talk about where they are from. I have learnt so much from my friends about the world we live in because I accept that we are all very different.

Why is your bum blue?

Ruslan and I have big blue birth marks on our bottoms. When I was born the doctor told my mum that mixed race children usually have a distinguishing birth mark somewhere on their body. The doctor also told my mum that these birth marks have to be documented so that they are not mistaken for bruises. These birth marks are called "Mongolian blue spots". Ruslan has one on his bum, but he also has one on the top of his right foot. Mum has told me that some mixed-race children have them everywhere on their bodies but that some of our spots will start to fade as we get older. Mine has already started to fade.

The End

Tendayi Oborn was born in Zimbabwe and has lived in Australia for more than 15 years. Tendayi is a hardworking Lawyer, Singer and Songwriter. Tendayi Chivunga is married to Martyn Oborn who co-owns their business Tee Legal and is a Miner by trade. Tendayi has excellent skills in identifying, understanding and addressing cross-cultural issues and issues facing people from culturally and linguistically diverse backgrounds. Tendayi has dedicated her career to social justice and ensuring that people from all backgrounds have access to justice and legal services. Tendayi has excelled as a reputable solicitor and runs her legal practice Tee Legal out of the coastal town Newcastle in New South Wales Australia. This book is based on Arnja Oborn and Ruslan Oborn, Tendayi and Martyn's rumbunctious, vivacious and adorable mixed race children.